ALL THE BROKEN BLOOM

Poems on Self-Love and Healing

September Stardust

All the Broken Bloom: Poems on Self-Love and Healing by September Stardust
Copyright © 2023 September Stardust
ISBN:
Paperback 978-621-479-487-4
eBook 978-621-479-485-0

Published by: 8Letters Bookstore & Publishing
Philippine Tel no: 0915 268 8718
International Tel no: +852 6690 5941
Website: www.8lettersbooks.com
Book layout by Cindy Wong

This book is for you

TABLE OF CONTENTS

BURROWING SEED

BOTANY

Sow seeds of self-love.
Blossom through the cracks
you once thought broke you.
Let flowers spring from jagged pathways
to reveal the beauty you've held back.
In this state of grace
from seed to stem
from root to fruit
from brokenness to beauty -
blossom without restraint.

AUTHOR

You are not a chapter in someone else's book.
You are a one-of-a-kind once-upon-a-time,
the creator of your own happily ever after.
When will your writing begin?

YOUR NAME IS YOUR VESSEL

Your name holds a thousand meanings.
It carries the turning of cultures.
It holds the shape of time.
You may not have chosen it,
but you can choose how to carry it.
What do you pour out of it?
What do you choose it to mean?

MARK

Believe
you are
unlike any other -
every mark you make
sings.

ASH

There is space for you in this world.
Earth awaits the warmth of your soles.
Fire kindles for your command.
Wind prepares at your cradling.
Water leans towards your becoming.
The thought of you enthralls all nature.
You are the child of the trees and skies.
Come make your presence known.

HOW STARS ARE BORN

See past all debris.
Amidst clouds and dust, you shine.
Trust the light in you.

UNRAVEL ME A GARDEN

There are peonies beneath your skin,
petals stretching flesh with fervor.
Roses bloom upon your fingers,
burgundy heady with
the potency you hold.
Wrapped around your limbs are lilies,
your grace manifesting
in silky white.
You leave behind a trail
of violets and posies,
fragrant truths unraveling the wonderful authentic you.

WITHIN YOU

You hold within you
colors undiscovered,
chapters unread,
stories untold,
words unwritten.

You hold within you
a powerful love
that transforms beauty to
beautiful purpose.

The cracks on your skin
are fragments flowers grow through.

You are blossoming.
Open your arms.
Bloom.

LETTER TO
MY YOUNGER SELF

Being quiet is not a weakness, little one.
Go read your books. Write your poems.
You do not need to run and play
the way other children do.
There is strength in finding comfort on your own.
This is called "solitude."
Go relish in the joy of being one with *you*.

GRATEFUL GLOW

Wash the day away with sage and lavender.
Wrap yourself in the softest robes.
Dab your wrists with rose petal oil.
Smell the aroma of invigorating cinnamon.
Meditate with garnet, ruby and moonstone.
Honor your temple. Cherish your soul.
Self-love does not have to be spoken to be heard.

STARDUST

Heed the stars' singing:
They call for you to fully stir
your stardust into being.

LOVE READING

What have you been denying yourself for so long?
Move on from the energy that shackles you.
Show love to parts of yourself you've been neglecting.
Take control of your happiness.
You deserve to start another journey.

TAKE HEART

Do not allow your past to drain you.
There is no joy in being enslaved by
what no longer serves you.
Only courage reaps rewards.

FOG

Make peace with the fog.
Sometimes it shows you
there are other ways
to move forward.

HOW I LEARNED TO BREATHE

Carefully, like unwrapping gifts
under Grandma's watchful eye -
we can still use the paper for later.

Tentatively, afraid to be alone -
so I say yes when I mean no.

Fiercely, hot oil on skin
making me gasp and realize -
the power in my lungs
is all mine.

DARKNESS AND LIGHT

Make peace with the shadows inside.
What claws at your soul can liberate you.
Darkness is there to remind you
you too carry light.
You are an eclipse.

SMOKE & MIRRORS

Tell yourself
what you're afraid of.
Peel away barriers
keeping you from
seeing the power of
the softer you.

FREE YOUR WILD

Banish fear.
Walk through fire.
Hound dark waters.
Free your wild.

THE CONSTANCY OF
THE MOON

The opal night speaks of change
but one thing is clear:
the moon - she stays.
In evenings one can't find her,
trust that she is there.
Oceans rise to greet her.
Even the sun needs her to breathe.

WINTER'S MELODY

She sings in snowstorms
unprepared to bloom.
She speaks in avalanches
refusing to blossom.
She weeps in hail
afraid of change.
The Sun understands -
she hears prayers in Winter's melodies
and gently says to
take her time.
The beauty of Spring
begins in her healing.

THE GRACE OF GRAY

Lean into the gray.
The rain doesn't hold the answers
but in the in-between of
drops falling and
mists forming
lies a silence that sings
all will be okay.

INTO THE FIRE

Surrender to the call
of your searching soul.
Barefoot-bold ballerina
tiptoeing across embers,
firm amidst fire
pulling at your skin.
You will not let pain win.
You are a phoenix-in-waiting,
primed to fly high.

SLOW AND STEADY

Move with the tides.
In and out.
In and out.
The ebb and flow
lulls you into a rhythm that
cradles and crashes.

You may not be there yet
but you are moving.
You are flowing.
You are carefully

cautiously

healing.

FLOWER

To watch her bloom in spring
is beautiful.
But to find her blossoming in winter
is breathtaking -
flowering despite snow
eating at her roots,
aiming her petals at the sun despite hail
shredding her leaves.

BEGIN AGAIN

This is what the ocean taught me -
that the castles we build are temporary
that the things we choose to say
can be washed away
and that this - this is okay
for we can start and build again.

UNFURLING

WAYS TO BLOOM

Run with half-tied shoelaces.
Walk out the door with wet hair.
Chase a cab while biting into a sandwich.
Skip the elevator and take the stairs.
Just keep moving, dear. Keep moving.
Even deeply buried seed keep pushing
till pavement cracks burst with blossoms.

ORIGAMI YOU

Fold and unfold,
transform tiny to great,
rehome grand to simple.
Flow and bend,
smooth out creases,
grow into your grooves.
Tuck and pleat
as your heart wishes.
You are who you
intend to be.

33

MAKE WAY

The greatest plans for you
are on the other side of the door.
How much of yourself is in the way?

BROKEN AND BRIGHT

While my mind tells me
having jagged lines and
cracked edges are
reasons to rebuild,
my heart assures me
being broken is just one way
to let more of my light
shine through.

Check one:
( ) Mind over heart
( ) Heart over mind

LOVE LETTER

Love letters for:
Him. Her. Them.
The one. The one that got away. The one that cannot be.
Friend. Soulmate. Lover.

Themes:
I can't live without him. She is my forever.
Their joy matters more than mine.
He is all love songs I drink to.
She is all what my wishes are made of.
They are poems I cannot write.

Return to Sender:
Your greatest love story is you.

PETALED POETRY

Draw from your inner well.
Feel the rooting of buds spreading, moving, growing.
Part your lips to the sky.
Watch all the flowers fly.
You were made to be a bearer of spring,
every word an awakening,
winged petals your poetry.

SWOON

Blush again,
this time with imaginings
entirely of honest thoughts
that have you swooning to
what now's.

UNCOCOONED

Promise yourself:
Cocoon no whispers.
Thread your way around
what shields you.
Look at life undefined.

THIS IS YOUR SIGN

Take the reading of these words as a sign:
You are homeward bound.
Every stumble is a nudge forward.
Every scream is a battle cry.
If it's a sign you seek, let this be it:
Pursue the significant you.

TO THE MOON

You may not carry the brightest light
but you have guided the lost in darkness.
We cannot all be the sun
still we shine in ways all our own.

BUTTERFLY

Say yes to yourself more.
You will get the transformation you deserve.

CHOOSE JOY

Joy is a risk that always pays off
even if it comes with a side of doubt and fear.
Take a chance with choices that make you happy.
You deserve to be elated.

DANDELION

You are a dandelion in bloom,
blossoming in quiet corners,
holder of hopes and wishes,
soon: guardians of the wind's whispers.

LOOKING GLASS

When was the last time
you looked into your eyes and
whispered tender words?

BLUSH AND BLOSSOM

Rise above the doubts
that cloud your
beautiful nakedness.
You are the rawness of spring,
ever budding,
ever blooming.

STARFLOWER

Embrace the way your petals open -
sunflower yellow, midnight crazed.
Whisper no apologies to the day
and leave no ghosts.
You were made to shine by starlight.

ROYAL

Have I told you

the world is worthy of your majesty?

Wear your crown.

Raise your scepter.

We are all born royal.

GOOD MORNING

Uncurl yourself to the morning's beckoning.
Be it a hushed salute or an unrestrained yawp,
kindle the day your way
for it is no one else's beginning but yours.

NO RUSH

Make peace with your body
slowly, carefully, gently.
Unlearn what other mirrors say
to see the beauty you hold
one scar at a time.

GALAXIAN

Stand tall.
Hold up the universe
on your shoulders
and feel yourself
take flight.
The galaxy you carry
is more powerful
when you believe.

KIND EYES

Love yourself with kind eyes,
crystal clear intentions,
sober confessions
spilling from pools of
black, blue, brown, gray, green.
You do not have to be naked
to be seen.

52

FUTURE YOU

Monogram tomorrows.
Versions of your life
are waiting to be
called forward.

CELESTINE

Selenite calm,
celestine wise,
the truths you spill
hold power.

SPRING AGAIN

Isn't it tiring, they always ask,
to unfurl petal after petal,
knowing they will pluck you
till you are left bare?
It's about loving, the flower answers,
every blooming is a beginning,
knowing my scent will linger,
long after the petals fall.

REBEL

She craves the moon
in a field of yellow dawns:
rebel sunflower.

CATCHING THE LIGHT

AWAKE

Hold your name sacrosanct.
Open your eyes to your authority.
Now watch how all the light
flows towards you.

CITRINE WILL

You carry the power of the sun.
Spread your arms and see
how much of life's fullness
flows because of you.
You are made of fresh beginnings.
Shine and manifest your greatness.

YOU ARE THE SUNRISE

Look at yourself
the way you look
at the sunrise -
with quiet reverence
and peaceful awe.

You are first light fresh,
softly golden.
Look closely -
how gentle you shine!

DAWNING

Open the connection between gut and heart.
Courage spills from this life bridge,
eager to reward with joys that come
only with intuition's gifts.
Watch your latent stories unravel.
Make space for this magic.

YOU ARE HERE

Make love to your life.
Romance how the wind whips your hair across your cheek.
Listen to the quiet buzz of the TV from the other room,
the rumbling of the truck outdoors, the humming of the electric
fan.
Warm the cold floor with your bare feet then walk outdoors
and feel the grass blades tickle your soles.
Inhale the beauty of presence.
Exhale your joy within.

LIONESS HEART

Listen to your lioness heart.
It beats for you to seize your heroine's path.
It throbs to unleash your elegant growling.
Quietly, loudly,
ROAR.

RIVER SOUL

Embrace the chameleon you.
Flow your river soul through seasons.
You are without niche nor genre
but of fluid flesh and time.

STARTING LINE

I claim my awakening.
I dance through doubt,
declaring there are no deadlines
to beginnings.

GOLDEN

Branches sprawl across my skin
golden-etched, soul-stretched,
beauty overflowing from
my budding heart.

SUPERNOVA

You are of certain uncertainties,
a gift of giving infinities.
Why do you color within the lines
when you are a universe
born from supernovas?

69

COLOR YOU ALIVE

Stain your skin with colors
that jolt your spirit into song.

STELLAR

Others shine bright
with your open heart
and soar even higher
when you fan your flames stellar.

BE THE LIGHT

Shine without apologies.
Shadows cower at your giving courage.
You are an abundance of untold stories
waiting to be written.

SUNSET

You wear the sunset well:
golden hour-kissed,
pastel peony-blushing.
You are the surreal made serene,
bathing everyone in your magic.

A POET'S CREED

Breathe life into
souls long haunted
by the heavy unsaid.

Crack open a
heavy earth bursting
with aching declarations.

Balm the landlocked
with primal magic found
in the history of roots.

Drip the poetry of blood
across all who need to
feel alive.

74

SUPERHERO

You hold the sun's power in your hands
the moon's kindness in your open arms.

ANDROMEDA

Your beauty is a threat
only to those who
don't believe in theirs.
They may chain you down
with their insecurities
but your elegant truth
cannot be shackled.
Shine, Andromeda. Shine.

SAKURA AGATE

Recover from yesterday's pain
by being present at every moment.
Refresh beginnings with a mindful heart.
You are the child of love and light.

LET'S PLAY

Play is the universe's love language.
Believe in the power of laughter.
Believe in the power of dreaming together.

RUBY

Your heart is ruby brave.
Pulse blood red for all
that makes you feel alive.
You are power. You are love.
You are ruby strong.

SWAYING STILL

SOVEREIGN

Take hold of your sovereignty.
In everything you do,
in everything you say,
how much of your power
are you giving away?

FLOW

Don't rush the answers.
Bend into what eases open.
Turn the pages slowly.
Slow dance with uncertainty.
Trust in the giving of time.
You will get there.
You're already on your way.

YOURS

Claim your space.
Own your place.
With respect, you flourish.
With openness, you grow.
Nobody gets to tell you
where you do or don't belong.

CRAVE YOURSELF

You have filled enough
of other people's cups.
Look into the galactic swirl
of your heart's spillings.
Steady the hands that
bring the cup to your lips.
Do not taste. *Ravish.*
Do not sip. *Devour.*
You are delicious grace
and magnificent madness.
Drink from your own cup
and be unafraid to
ask for more.

EARTH BROWN

Dig your roots deep.
Sway to all that they say
but stand true to the virtues
you hold to be true.
Loving yourself
stains your hands
earth brown.

86

BLUE

All the shades of blue
bloom beautifully - each one
bears a light within.

YOUR LIGHT, YOUR POWER

Protect the light in you
with the fierceness of a storm
reminding the world of her power.

UNCHAINING

Andromeda tells me
she could have saved herself.
Sometimes monsters aren't tamed
by the sharpest of swords
but the calmness of time.
This is how the ocean heals.

FRAGMENTS

In each of your breaking,
discover a piece of yourself
worth keeping.

COMPLETE

Marry the thought between "fullness" and "you".
Someone else won't make you whole.
Only you complete you.

STAY

Someone's world
became a better place
because of you.
Someone's life
changed for good
because of you.
No single life
is disconnected
from another
even when
we feel most alone.
Stay
and let the world experience
how much good
there is
that comes
from you.

CONQUER

You're a fighter.
Look at this valley you're in
not as a slump
or a dip
or a lull
but as respite
as recovery
as springboard
to getting you higher
propelling you forward.
Every conqueror rests too.

SIMPLY

Take away all complications
of dictates, expectations,
and you're left
with love,
simply love,
and don't we all need
so much more of that?

LOVE ME FREE

It is in loving myself
that I am free.
I have tucked rose quartz
into my heart's nooks,
tiny badges of courage
nudging, igniting,
releasing, pursuing,
going, going, going,
glowing.

YOU ARE A RIVER

They watch you flow,
chiding your lack of firmness,
naming it weakness.

But don't they see?

You are a river.
Your strength is the current
carrying life from streams to seas.

To be resolute doesn't need the
pounding of a fist or the
raising of a voice.

Let them watch you be unwavering
with mercurial grace.

FLOWER CROWN

She will not count the petals
nor play odd or even games
to know if she is loved or not.
She weaves herself a crown and says,
"The loving starts with me."

PROPHET'S SONG

Trust in the power of your quiet love.
It cups kindness words can't speak enough of.
Trust in the strength of your soft voice.
It holds echoes that drown out all the noise.
Trust in the greatness of your timid you.
You carry courage that will see you through.

QUIET HEART

My quiet is a gift.
It is the calm that grounds me
when the world gets too loud,
when we all need to lean into the lull.
It is the hush before the push
when we need to find the power in the pause,
when we all just need to listen.

SEE ME IN MY ENTIRETY

I am a million fragments,
a million flames,
my entirety a mosaic
of subtle hues
boldly saying
I am here.
I choose to stay.

RIDING THE WIND

REHOMING

This is my rehoming:
I bare my fullest me
to the changing of seasons
without fear of
getting lost again.

BEAUTIFUL TRUTHS

How much of yourself can you
hold in your hands and declare,
"This. This is beautiful."?

(This. This is a trick question.)

Every soft curve and bend - beautiful.
Every sweet roll and ridge - beautiful.

There is all of yourself you can
hold in your hands and declare,
"I. I am beautiful."

(This. This is your beautiful truth.)

REACQUAINTED

I am getting reacquainted with my body.
This, the swelling of my belly,
carrier of life and instinct.
This, the curve of my behind,
plump and feline graceful.
This, the scar on my breast,
brooch of immeasurable strength.
This, my creased hands,
wands for written healing.
This, the hollow of my throat,
gateway of this braver voice.
Hello. I'm so happy to meet you again.

HOW TO FORGIVE YOURSELF

Send yourself a bouquet of tulips with an
"Everything will be okay" card. /
Pat yourself and say, "There, there."

Take a long shower, emerge with
lavender-scented self-love. /
Splash your face with ice cold water,
open your eyes refreshed.

Sleep. Sit. Crawl. Stay still.
Walk. Run. Dance. Be in motion.

Listen to what your soul
doesn't seem to be saying /
has always been saying.

Forgive. / Forgive.

STARSEED

I am many lives beating with one celestial heartbeat.
Dusk bears the same message: Home is near.
The way forward is at the intersection of memory and presence.
Memory {I am seven years old standing under a canopy of
bougainvillea
knowing I have been here before}:
Presence {I am reawakening to many possible beginnings}
I am a stellar being finding her way home.

INTO THE OPEN SEA

Let me flow into your open mouth.
With vulnerability, I surrender.
With trust, I hope.

WHOLEHEARTED

Remember this - you are enough.
You are love and you are light.
Love yourself wholeheartedly.
Feel yourself take flight.

TOAST

Toast
to joys hidden in shadows
to songs you have yet to sing
to streets waiting to be crossed
Toast
to seeing beginnings in endings
to awakening from slumber
to drying the tears
Toast
to tomorrow's presents.

TRANSIENT DOVE

Fly even with a heavy heart.
Widen your wings,
every inch opened
a prayer from the grateful.
Soar ballerina graceful,
blessed with Sun's kiss
and Moon's nodding.
Any journey could end
with the next sunrise.
Today, let's ride the wind
paper light.

SOFT LANDINGS

Move with the reserved ease
of petals caught in a breeze.
Trust you will land
somewhere soft
like the cradling of
"I have found you."

FALLING VIOLETS

Love yourself fiercely
with all fragility.
Hold yourself with
the serenity of
falling violets.
The softer you cup
yourself in your hands,
the longer you will
love yourself boldly.

NEW YEAR DECLARATIONS

May this year's scars prove to you:
You have broken through.
Wild in spirit,
strong in heart,
the broken can dance too.

LESSONS FROM THE WIND

Love without abandon.
In your trail leave a scent of soft and sweet.
Let seedlings grow from tenderness left behind.
Do not apologize for uncaged passion.
It is in your mad gusts
dead leaves are swept away
and paths are cleared for those
who have the strength to stay.

BRIAR ROSE TODAY

Heavy sleeper with big dreams.
Wakes up to her own kisses.
Conquered fear of spindles
through thorn-lined adventures.
Believes it's not the end of the world
despite spells that feel a century-long.
Dreams of her prince and/or princess but
fights her own dragons.

WINGED GLORY

Thunder your heart, golden.
You are winged glory,
majestic wisdom in flight.
Your tenderness flames others' spirits
even from afar.

REVEL

Dress yourself with no restrictions.
Paint your lips carnelian red.
Shadow your eyes gold.
You are lotus flower pure,
primrose calm, marigold joyful.
Revel in the goddess you are.

WORTHY

Never wear your worth
as if it were a borrowed crown.

EMBRACE YOUR UNTAMING

Untame your wild.
Steer the wind you ride.
You are the Universe's child -
nebula gentle, galaxian strong.
Receive the spirits' gifts.
Exhale the legacy of your soul.
You are love unbridled.

WITH ALL HONESTY

I am home in the swelling of my curves;
branches that stretch along my hips
golden in the abandoning of stirring flesh,
softness around the dip of my waist
graceful in its circling, riding, swaying.
I am home in my body's honeyed way
of knowing the certainty of my desires,
the honesty of my fire.

ALL THE BROKEN BLOOM

I will not be bound by pretty pots or landscaped greens.
My spirit soars beyond prescribed perimeters and rigid rules.
I will flower through the pavement cracks.
I will bear fruit in swamp and shade.
I will blossom in the darkness.
All the broken bloom.

THIS IS HOW I BLOOM

COMPLETE THE FOLLOWING POEM YOUR WAY.

THIS IS HOW I BLOOM

I am handwritten (your favorite flower in plural) on paper (mode
of transportation in plural),
unread (book genre in plural) on bedside (furniture in plural).

I am (your favorite season) stories and (body of water) dreams,
(your favorite color) (your favorite word in plural) and (your
favorite weather) skies.

I am glass (something you build in plural) and wooden (your
favorite part of the house in plural),
naked (your favorite part of your body) on (kind of fabric)
evenings.

I am (your preferred level of noise) (a favorite thing you read in
plural)
tucked in (your second favorite color) (your favorite landform in
plural),
written to be read again.

ACKNOWLEDGEMENTS

With thanks to:

My family and friends, for reading my poems through the years and cheering me on.

My Mama, for unlocking the healing world of writing for me with the gift of "A New Treasure of Children's Poetry" when I was seven years old.

The 8Letters team, for being wonderful and supporting me through the process.

My forever love, for finding me and keeping me found.

And finally, to you, dearest reader, for joining me on this journey from seed to blossom. I hope this book nurtures your greatness, and that these poems help you bloom in any space, in any place, in any season, and in your own beautiful way.

ABOUT THE AUTHOR

September Stardust writes of self-love, healing, and the vulnerability in loving others. She is a poet based in the Philippines. You may find more of her poetry on IG: september.stardust.

Author Portrait: Ennarova